Restoring Dolls — a practical guide

Restoring Dolls
— a practical guide

Doreen Perry

Bishopsgate Press Ltd.
37 Union Street, London SE1 1SE

Acknowledgement

I would like to thank Mrs Ida Daniels for loaning dolls and dolls clothes to be used for illustration both in this book and for the jacket, also my assistant Miss Susan Cartwright who has helped the production of this book in many ways.

© 1985 Bishopsgate Press Ltd

ISBN 0 900 873 59 0 (cased)
0 900 873 61 2 (limp)

All enquiries and requests relevant to this title should be sent to the publisher, Bishopsgate Press Ltd., 37 Union Street, London, SE1 1SE

Printed by Whitstable Litho Ltd., Millstrood Road, Whitstable, Kent.

Contents

Introduction

It is seldom these days that one finds dolls in pristine condition. In the event of such a discovery one also has to find a great deal of money to pay for them. Such dolls are an extremely good investment, as well as giving so much pleasure to their proud owners.

However, for those of us who cannot avail themselves of such treasures, the search goes on for the broken, worn and dirty dolls with missing or damaged limbs. These are worth investing in as they also accrue in value, but to a lesser degree than their grander counterparts. One will not only have the satisfaction of improving such sad mementoes of yester-year, but also obtain a good bargain.

Now a word of warning to all would-be restorers. Do resist the urge to over-restore, thereby losing the doll's authenticity. A damaged or dirty doll will obviously benefit from being gently cleaned and repaired sufficiently to prevent any further deterioration. This also applies to wigs and clothes, as well as to the doll itself. If you want it to look as if it has just been manufactured, you may as well buy a reproduction. A careless restoration can detract from the value, rather than enhance it.

It is a good idea to build up a stock of spare parts. One can buy limbs, old eyes, and other odd parts from junk shops, flea markets, and, of course, doll and juvenilia fairs. These stand-bys can prove invaluable and save time in authentic restoration. One can also marry parts together, making complete dolls. It can be very satisfying for a collector if a whole doll is achieved out of bits and pieces. The harm in this is if the doll is eventually sold to some unsuspecting buyer. This marrying is easier to spot as one gets more involved in repairing, but do be on your guard for it.

The repairs mentioned in this book will range from Victorian dolls and up to and including the vinyl dolls of today. In these days of built-in obsolescence, the modern dolls are mentioned only briefly, as they are not so easy to repair, although even some of these have become collectors' items. The antique dolls are dealt with in more depth, as not only are they easier to repair, but their higher value makes it more worthwhile to spend time and money on them. However, it is equally rewarding for a restorer to see the pleasure a restored antique doll gives to a collector, or to see the sheer delight of a little girl whose 'favourite doll has been made better.'

It must be said that there is a great variety of damage which can happen to dolls of any age and this is restorable by a multitude of methods. In this book it is only possible to cover the restoration which is most common and also the most manageable for a learner to attempt. When the student restorer has achieved the methods described here then he or she can move on to further reading, a list of which is given at the end of the book, and to experiment to find new ways.

Dolls' hospitals existed in every town at one time but today they are extremely rare. Therefore it is hoped that with the aid of this book you will become your own doll doctor, and that you will derive much pleasure and satisfaction in so doing.

Repairing Heads

Before you start to repair a damaged head, it is important that you recognize the materials from which it is made.

Bisque heads: These heads are easily recognized by the fact that they have a matt or 'biscuit' finish. Some even have a lifelike bloom on them. They come in all sizes from toddler to miniature for dolls houses. Basically the main ingredients are uniform but, as in a favourite cooking recipe the chefs, or in the case of dolls the manufacturers, would have added something extra to make their dolls heads different to their competitors.

Although the firing and finishing would not vary, the actual end product could be very different. You have only to feel the finish with the tips of your fingers to check how it differs. Also, when it comes to re-glazing, you will notice that no two flesh tints are the same.

China or glass heads: These are the highly glazed heads in white porcelain, with rosy cheeks, painted eyes and moulded hair (usually black or blonde). These vary in size from large to miniatures.

Parian heads: These are neither glazed nor flesh coloured, but in common with china or glass heads they have painted eyes and moulded hair. Occasionally these dolls are found with glass eyes and hair but they are extremely rare.

Painted china: These are easily recognized by the fact that the paint can be scratched. In fact, lifting the wig usually takes off the paint from around the hair line. Although not as valuable as the others, one can find some attractive dolls of this type.

1. Bisque heads

2. China or glass heads

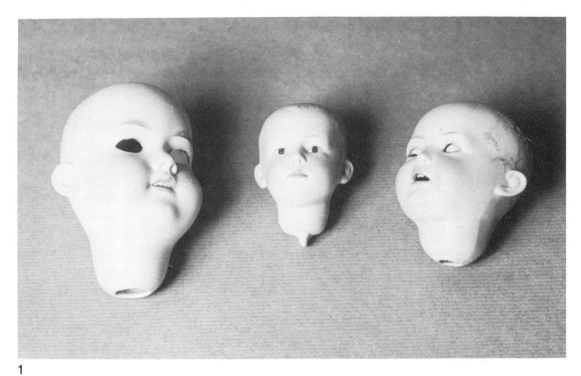

1

2

Pot heads: These are heavier than bisques and china heads and of a much coarser appearance. The materials used vary greatly with the make but are generally of a terra cotta type. These dolls usually have moulded hair and are painted. Pot heads are sometimes confused with better quality composition heads but the heavy weight of the pot head should give it away.

Wax heads: The first kind is where wax has been poured into a mould which makes a solid head. These are recognized by the slightly pugilistic effect on the features that age and wear produce. Secondly there is wax over composition. This is where papier-machés, composition, or similar materials are dipped into liquid wax to form a thin coating. These can be recognized because the coating of wax tends to crackle or craze and is of course lighter than the solid wax head. Wax heads can have moulded hair or real hair and quite often the most beautiful glass eyes.

Composition heads: The term composition covers a multitude of materials from papier-maché to the better quality compressed materials containing glue, cardboard, sawdust, and even some with clay in their content. These heads are always painted, sometimes with glass or synthetic eyes, and in some cases painted eyes. One mostly finds baby dolls with composition heads, although I have seen some charming toddler and adult dolls. These heads can crackle and craze very badly and in some instances the paint lifts away from the compressed surface.

3. A parian head

4. A painted china head. Notice that some of the paint has peeled off at the hairline

3

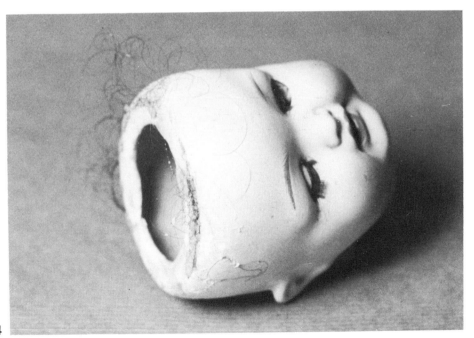

4

5. *A pot head*

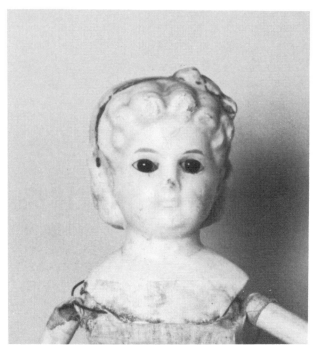

6. *A wax head*

12

7. *Composition head*

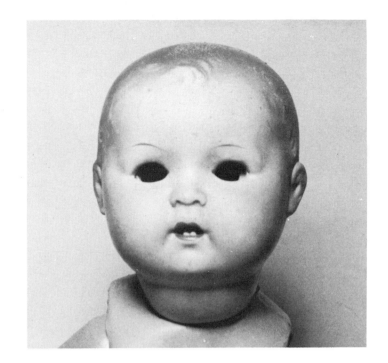

8. *Celluloid head*

Plastic and vinyl heads: Plastic heads are rigid as opposed to vinyl ones which are softer and more pliable. They are found with moulded hair, synthetic or mohair wigs or rooted hair. These are not usually worth restoring unless they are a precious favourite or rather exceptional as they are usually quite modern. It is very likely cheaper to buy a new doll.

9. Rigid plastic heads

Celluloid heads: These can be found with moulded hair or real or synthetic hair and in all sizes. They can have painted or glass eyes. The toddler and baby dolls usually have celluloid bodies, but the better quality heads can be found on kid or fabric bodies and usually with celluloid hands and arms. They are much lighter to hold but they can be easily crushed, and are best kept away from fire or heat, as they can easily ignite. They are described as indestructible, but in fact they are very easily destroyed. Some types of celluloid can become extremely brittle and will crack very easily. Most of these dolls were made during the 1920s and 1930s.

10. Vinyl heads. Note how the hair is rooted in

14

9

10

Taking Down an Old Repair (This method is suitable for china, pot, bisque and parian heads).

The common fault one finds is that amateur restorers tend to use far too much glue when sticking the pieces together, thereby failing to obtain neat fine joins and with the pieces of head fitting together well. See illustration one — an example of a badly stuck head.

Firstly remove all additions, e.g. eyes, tongue, teeth and wigs. With a long-handled coarse paint brush, paint nitromors along the existing cracks, pushing it well into the old glue and working it in throughly (illustration two). Let it soak in for 5–10 minutes, then place it in a bowl or sink of very hot water (almost boiling). WARNING — if nitromors gets on to skin, wash the affected area immediately under the cold water tap.

Extra special care has to be taken with painted china heads. Work on the inside only, otherwise the existing paint will be removed and you will have to repaint the entire head. With luck the repair should come apart. If not, one can endeavour to break it apart with the fingers or the pointed end of a spatula. If this is not successful, repeat the process again until the china comes apart. Do not be timid about this, as a certain amount of force can be used. A more drastic method which can be used 'if all else fails' is to boil the head after an application of nitromors.

When all the pieces are apart, use a scalpel blade or spatula to scrape and clean the old glue thoroughly from the edges, and then clean the edges with steel wool.

All edges must be thoroughly clean otherwise you will not get a good join when regluing.

11. *A badly stuck head. Note the thick unsightly joins and a piece locked out*

12. *Painting the cracks with Nitromors prior to taking the head apart*

13. *The head has come apart after painting with Nitromors and being placed in hot water*

14. *Cleaning the edges thoroughly with steel wool to ensure that no particles of dirt or glue remain*

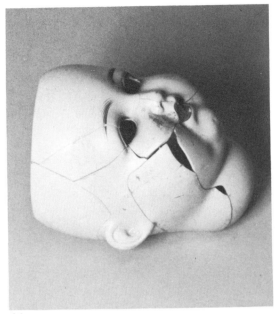

11

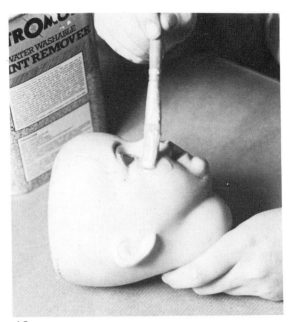

12

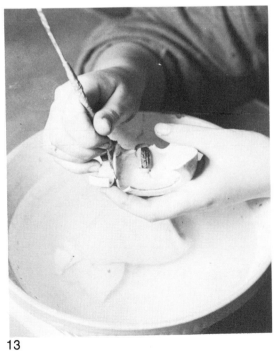

13

14

The Art of Sticking

When all the pieces are quite clean it is wise to fit them together dry (without glue) to ensure that they are all there and that there are no fitting problems. This is especially necessary in the case of a multi-broken head. When you are satisfied that all is in order take the head apart again and prepare the glue.

Mix your 'Araldite', remembering to mix the hardener to the resin in equal quantities. Prepare strips of masking tape or sellotape. Carefully spread 'Araldite' on one edge only of each piece. It is important not to use too much, because if you do you will find that the glue will ooze out as soon as you put two edges together. This makes a messy job and an insecure bond. Place masking tape on both of the sides that you are joining, so they you can press the join together, at the same time pushing masking tape over the join with your thumbs. This binds the join together, but can be moved if you wish to improve the join.

The same rules apply to the super epoxy fast-drying glue, but I do not advise you to use this on a head with more than one or two joins, as you will have difficulty in moving the pieces if you wish to improve the join.

Substitute 'Evostick' wood glue when sticking **composition** or **wax heads**. Clean any surplus glue away with methylated spirit or thinners. Do be careful, when repairing more than two broken pieces, that you do not lock a piece out. (see illustration 3). If a piece to be stuck is an awkward shape, it can be placed in a tray of sand at an appropriate angle, or supported by plasticine. Leave joined pieces in a supported position to dry for twenty-four hours.

15. *When the head is broken as badly as this it should be assembled first with sticky tape to make sure that there are no pieces missing*

16. *Joins being held together with tape to ensure that they will bond securely and neatly*

17. *These awkwardly shaped pieces are propped up in sand while the glue dries*

15

16

17

It is possible to stick **celluloid** and **plastic,** but as the cracks cannot be filled (which is dealt with in the next chapter), I feel it is worth mentioning two alternatives.

In the case of **celluloid,** hold the edges of the crack together and gently paint on acetone with a cotton bud. Acetone is a solvent which will melt the surface of the celluloid, therefore joining the two edges together. Similarly, you can hold the edges of plastic or vinyl together and close the join by melting the edges together using a very hot steel knitting needle. If either of these methods are used, please take the utmost care, as it is easy to do more damage. No repair done this way will be invisible.

18.   *The head completely restuck*

19.   *A cracked celluloid head which has been repaired by using acetone to fuse the parts together*

18

19

Filling and Building Up

For a beginner 'Milliput' is one of the easiest fillers to use. It comes in two sticks, a resin and a hardener. Equal quantities of each are mixed together until the marble effect disappears. The two sticks are different colours and should be mixed or kneaded with the fingers until the overall colour is even.

With a scalpel or spatula, pull the filler across the join from the lower side to the higher side. You can feel this with the tips of your fingers. Check this constantly as the levels will change along the length of the join.

When using the filler, take great care not to leave hard ridges and bumps. If you do you will regret this later when you come to rubbing down. Leave the filler to dry for twenty-four hours. It is essential that you obtain a smooth finish. Any fault at this stage will be accentuated rather than covered up.

When rubbing down start with the coarsest sandpaper, graduating to the finer papers. This process will probably have to be repeated several times until a really smooth finish has been achieved.

Another filler which may be used is 'Araldite' with titanium dioxide added. This is a much harder filler, but the process of filling and building up is the same as before. 'Araldite' is mixed as usual, and the titanium dioxide is added to the glue to make a soft but dry paste, pliable to use, but not too sticky. This last filler is not suitable for **composition** heads.

20. *The materials and tools required for filling and building up*

21. *Putting Milliput across the crack*

22. *A head which has been filled with Milliput but before rubbing down*

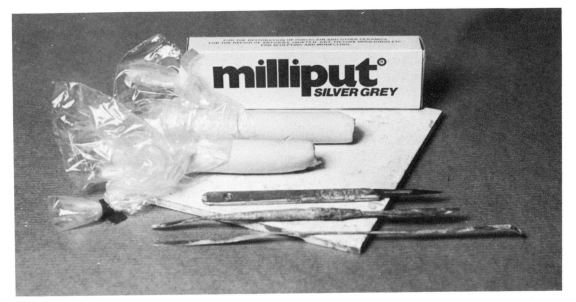

20

21

22

Wax Heads. Do not be too ambitious when repairing **wax heads.** Only attempt the simplest repair.

Probably the easiest way to repair a broken wax or wax over composition head is to rejoin the pieces using a wood adhesive. In this way they can be glued together exactly as described for the other types of heads. A solid wax head can also be joined with heat using a hot knitting needle or spoon to melt the wax before placing the two parts together.

If you need to fill a hole caused by a missing piece of wax this is quite possible. First select a suitable wax or wax mixture; I like to use beeswax, paraffin wax and ordinary candle wax mixed to suit the particular head which is being repaired. When you are happy with the wax it should be heated until molten and then dripped carefully into the hole. As the wax cools it should be smoothed down with a warm spoon handle to fit well with the original wax.

23. *The filled head (which is shown in illustations 21 and 22) rubbed down and ready for painting and glazing*

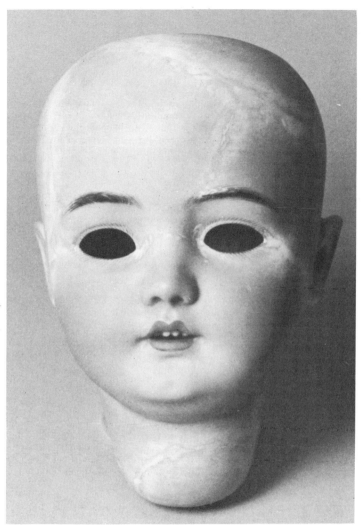

23

Re Glazing and Painting

This applies only to, **bisque, china or glass heads, parian, painted china, pot heads** and **composition.**

Dealing with **bisque** and **parian** first; remember to use a matt paint and mix your colours in a palette until you achieve the correct shade. When you think that the colour is correct dab a little on a piece of paper and hold it next to the head. Keep doing this until you are quite happy with the colour. If the repair is small a dab with your finger may be sufficient to cover it. At all costs you want to avoid hard lines or brush strokes showing when the paint has dried. To cover larger areas you could try dabbing the colour on with cotton wool or a sponge, or again with your fingers. I often paint with my fingers to smooth on the paint. You will of course use a very fine brush for lips, nostrils and eye lashes and be sure to complete all the painting and allow it to dry before you set it with a coating of matt varnish.

All other heads are painted with a gloss paint. Again you can apply paint with your fingers or with brushes. It is much better to use several coats of thin paint and gradually build up the colour. If you use the paint too thickly to start with you will end up with a hard line at the edge of your repair. Between each application of paint allow it to dry and then lightly rub down with flexigrit. Finish off with gloss or satin varnish according to the depth of the glaze.

If you have invested in an air brush, you will find that you do not have such a problem with brush marks or hard lines. However it is still best to build up the colour gradually by using thin layers of paint. Although you can cover the surface more evenly you may overspray lips

24. *This head has been painted in a contrasting colour for the benefit of the photograph to show the manner of the paintwork*

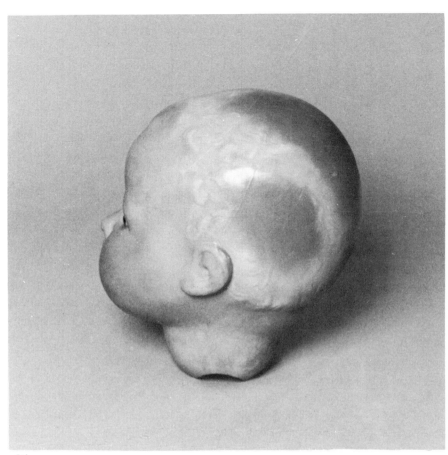

24

and eyebrows; if this happens wait until the paint is thoroughly dry and then carefully scrape back the paint with a scalpel as if you were painting. Do this between each coat in order to avoid hard lines.

Unless a repair has been necessary to the eyebrows, lips or eye sockets you should not need to repaint any of these with this method. It is possible to use a masking liquid, but I do not recommend this because you can again make hard lines around these areas. It would however be possible to use this method on lips.

Again finish off with a varnish according to requirement which can also be sprayed on with the air brush.

25. *A finished head showing the reglazed outer side*

26. *The same head showing the reglazed parts on the inside before the repair was completed*

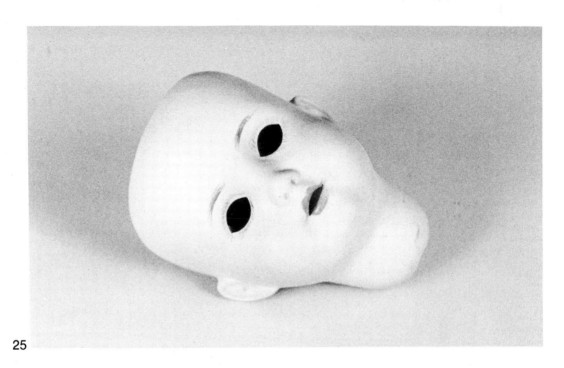

25

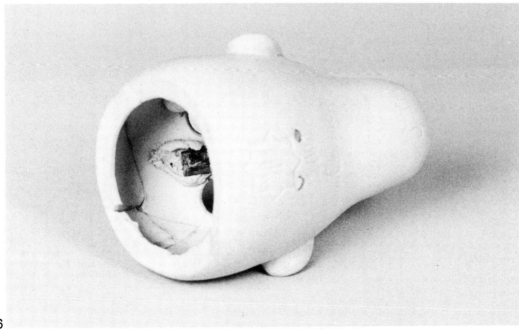

26

Wigs

Wigs are made of the following materials – real hair, dynel, nylon and mohair, and they can be bought ready made in a variety of styles. This is necessary when your doll has no hair at all. If it has any remains of the original you should try to work with this. Always choose a wig that is compatible with the doll. For example a doll manufactured in 1875 would never have worn a nylon wig; it would have worn either real hair or mohair according to the quality of the doll. Neither would you put a long wig or ringlets on a baby or toddler doll; they wear straight pudding basin or short curly styles. Ready made wigs cannot usually be altered into any other style, but this does not usually present a problem as there are so many styles available from which to choose.

When buying or making a wig do not forget that you will need a fibre board pate or dome. Some domes have a central hole which is used for top knot wigs (described later on).

If you feel ambitious enough to attempt making your own wigs, I have listed below a few simple styles, which are suitable for real hair or mohair.

The Strip Wig: First you need a piece of ribbon or tape matching as closely as possible the colour of hair; although when completed the ribbon will barely show. For a centre parting you need equal lengths of hair or mohair, so that it falls on either side of the ribbon (see illustration). Double over the ends of the hair and then glue or sew them under so that you now have what looks like a parting. For the back hair comb it down as in the illustration. You can make the same wig with a side parting. In this case one side of the hair must be longer than the other.

27. Strip wigs

28. Pates

30

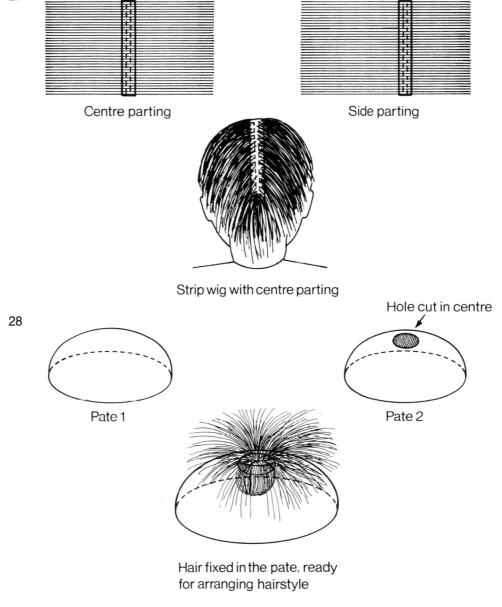

27

Centre parting

Side parting

Strip wig with centre parting

28

Pate 1

Hole cut in centre

Pate 2

Hair fixed in the pate, ready
for arranging hairstyle

This strip wig is suitable for any length of hair, and can be left in bunches for which a centre parting is best. I prefer a centre parting for a plaited style but I have also made plaited wigs with a side parting.

Once you have mastered the making of this wig style you can vary the design by adding a fringe, plaiting and coiling it and adding a bun or ear phones. The **Edwardian cottage loaf** style is also simple enough to prepare; arrange the hair as previously stated but comb the hair down over the face as well as down the back, as illustrated, then sweep the hair up evenly to the crown and fix by stitching into place.

Top knot wigs are only found on small dolls. Push the hair through hole, and fix on the under side by turning the ends over and stitching this is to make a knob of hair so that it will not slip through the hole. You can then drape or dress the hair over the crown according to preference.

29. A top knot wig

Restoring Old Wigs

It is always best to try to refurbish the original wig, rather than replace with a new one. To do this successfully takes a great deal of time and patience.

Removing The Wig

Usually the glue holding a wig on to the head is so old and brittle, that one can pull the wig away by hand, if not, one can insert (very carefully) a fine scalpel or blade under the glue, taking care not to cut or tear the fabric. Insert it in such a way that the blade is touching the porcelain. Quite often the fabric is rotten, but with care it is possible to refurbish.

It is also possible to wash wigs using tepid water only with a little Stergene or Fairy Liquid. Swish the wig in the water for two to three minutes then do the same in a bowl of clean water to rinse. Squeeze gently and replace

29

on the head to dry; this keeps the fabric base in shape and prevents shrinking. When dry, you can either remove the wig or leave it on the head to comb out. It is possible that the hair may have tangles. These will have to be teased out using a coarse tooth comb (a dog comb is useful). Gradually comb the hair starting from the ends, not from the crown.

When the hair is tangle free, dampen the hair if you wish to curl it. I prefer to use old fashioned rags instead of rollers, as they are softer and less damaging. However there is no harm in using rollers if you are careful. A slight smear of vaseline cold cream or vita point on the comb gives the hair a nice sheen.

You cannot comb mohair so before washing it tease out as many tangles as possible with the pointed end of a styling comb. It tends to become matted when wet. Wash it in tepid water and Stergene but do not swish it around. Instead hold it on the palm of your hands under the water patting it from one hand to the other. Rinse it in the same way.

30. *Combing out an old wig commencing at the ends of the hair*

Do not squeeze but lay it flat on a towel with another towel on top and press the water out. Leave it to dry out naturally. You may find that pieces of glue adhere to the mohair, pick these off with tweezers.

Re-stick the wig to the head and brush it gently; a baby brush is the most suitable for this. When gluing wigs the most suitable adhesive these days is Copydex.

34

30

Rooted Hair

You find rooted hair in wax dolls and this is usually real hair which is embedded into the warm wax. This can be done one strand at a time using a hot bodkin needle. One must take great care in doing this.

Then to the other extreme rooted hair is found in the plastic and vinyl dolls. It is possible to re-root a whole head but this would be very time consuming.

However if the head is patchy, or if you want to attempt a whole head the procedure is as follows. You will need a Tailor Marker (obtainable from dressmaker suppliers) which is a hollow needle and tube.

Punch holes in the head with a large size needle, in the same positions as the original holes. This will make them slightly larger and easier to use. Take five or six strands of hair about six inches or longer, wet the ends and thread them through a marker from the large end so that half the hair is on one end of the needle and half is on the other end. Push the marker into the hole and pull out slowly; the hairs will be doubled over and about 1/2 inch will remain in the head. When you have completed the head or have filled in the bald patch, brush the inside of the head with glue which will hold the hairs in place. When the glue has dried trim the hair if necessary.

31. *The outside of a head showing the punctured holes and the first row of hairs already implanted*

32. *The inside of a head ready to be glued*

33. *The marker for inserting hair*

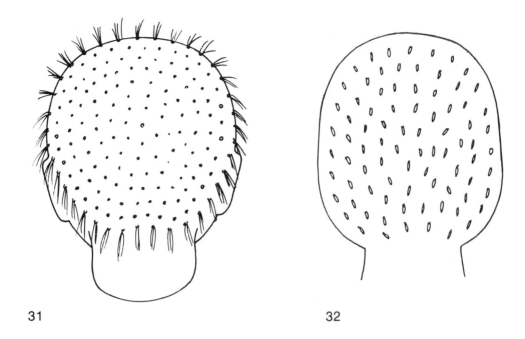

31   32

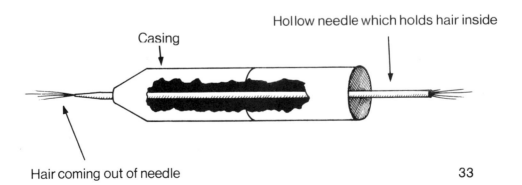

Casing

Hollow needle which holds hair inside

Hair coming out of needle

33

Teeth and Tongues

The original teeth in Victorian dolls were made in porcelain separately from the head; tongues were then sometimes added in plaster or felt. These were then mounted on a bar inside the head.

It is possible to buy these old originals at fairs and from dealers. New porcelain or plastic teeth are also available from suppliers and fairs. The teeth are usually on a bar in two's, three's, or four's.

Sometimes teeth in the mouth are broken but it is possible to repair these successfully with white Milliput. You sculpt this material directly onto the chipped or broken teeth and then carefully rub down to achieve the right finish. These are then repainted and reglazed before being fixed back into the head.

34. *Three arrangements of teeth*

35. *A rubber tongue on metal strip*

36. *A felt tongue*

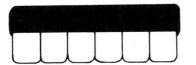

34

Baby teeth

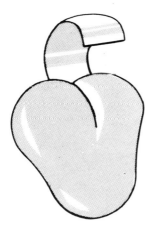

35

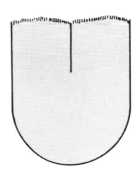

36

Eyes

Usually if the eyes are loose or lost this indicates that they were of the rocker type. They are held in place by plaster, which sometimes shrinks or is displaced or damaged allowing the eyes to fall out. If the plaster is still in place and the eyes fit back easily remember that they will fall out just as easily again. So carefully build more plaster onto the existing pieces, taking care not to inhibit the eye's natural movement, but shaping the plaster around the eye. You will have to keep checking the plaster, as it must not dry out completely but must be dry enough to enable you to manually move the rocker up and down. This must be done very gently as eventually the eyes should move freely on their own. When you are satisfied with the movement and they are secure, leave the plaster to dry out.

To make a new pair of rocking eyes, first line the eye socket on the inside of the head with doll wax. Place the round blown glass eyes onto this so that they will be held into place by the wax, although you can move the eyes until you are satisfied with their position. The wax is sold in small blocks, and is quite hard but will soften very quickly when kneaded between the fingers.

When the eyes are positioned correctly you are ready to make the T bar. Measure the width between the two eyes, plus the length of the wire required to finish at the weight. You will need two identical lengths of wire. Thread the two pieces of wire through the hole in the weight and bend the end of the wire to keep the weight from slipping off. (Weights can be purchased from fishing tackle shops). Now twist the wires together making the upright of the T. Bend the wires to make the cross part of the T. Bend the ends of each wire into eye holes, and at this stage you can see the eye mechanism taking shape.

37. The eyes set in wax in the sockets

38. Plaster now covers all of the eyes and the wax

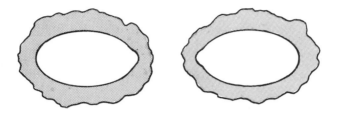

37

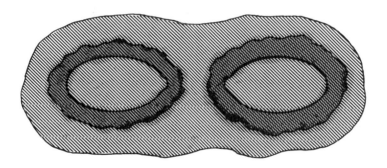

38

Mix plaster thickly so that it does not ooze into the hollow eyes but binds around the wire and effectively fixes the wire into the eyes and leave this plaster to dry thoroughly. Melt the sticky wax and with a spatula drop it carefully over the plaster until it is completely covered; several applications will be necessary. When this is hardened you can now remove your pair of rocking eyes and clean the wax from the eye socket. Mark on the glass part of the eye where you want the eye lids, melt the pink wax which comes in thin sheets until it is quite transparent, paint on to marked area and let it dry.

If you wish to attempt eye lashes you can embed them before the wax hardens. You will then have to apply another coating of wax to cover the ends and this is applied in the same way.

Now to set your rockers, and replace them in the head. Lightly vaseline the sides of the eyes where the plaster will hold them in place. Mix your plaster, so that it is sufficiently malleable to drop either from a teaspoon or wide spatula to mould around the eyes. It must not be too wet so that it spreads into sockets. You must constantly check the plaster whilst it is drying, Lift the rockers gently so that they move smoothly, and eventually they should rock freely by themselves; now leave plaster to dry thoroughly. To finish the job place a small piece of cork or wood in position so that the weight rests on it in both positions either open or shut.

Fixed Eyes
To fix the eyes in the head place the eyes in the socket on to a bed of wax to hold them in position, as in the previous instructions. Mix the plaster and pile it on to the eyes and leave to dry.

When dry, take a sharp pointed scalpel or knife and trim away any excess wax from the front of the eyes.

39. *The eyes set in wax in the sockets*

40. *Making the T-bar*

41. *The finished set of eyes*

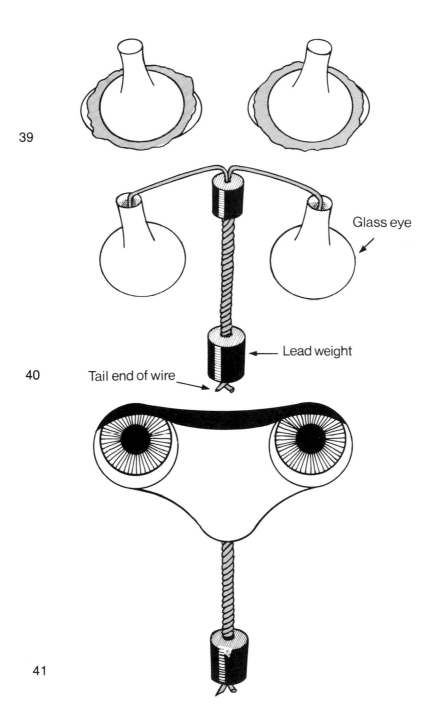

39

40

Glass eye

Lead weight

Tail end of wire

41

Modern Eyes

For dolls made in the 1930s and 1940s the eyes can be purchased ready made. They are of standard sizes and only need gluing into place.

For vinyl and plastic dolls the eyes can be purchased in pairs. They are two separate eyes, which are not on T bars. These eyes fit into a socket and unlike the other dolls the restorer works from the outside.

To remove the old eyes, hold the head over the steam of a kettle to warm the vinyl or plastic which makes it more pliable. If you try to remove them when the plastic is cold you could cause the eye socket to split. When the head is heated it should then be possible to dig out the eyes with a pointed but blunt instrument.

The same procedure with steam is repeated when inserting the new eyes except these are gently pushed into the sockets, and you may need to straighten them with the pointed instrument. Do make sure however, to keep the head warm whilst doing this.

42. Modern eyes

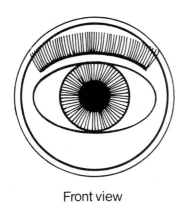

Front view

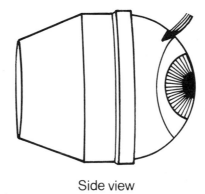

Side view

42

Heads — Two special Exercises

Example 1. When large pieces of the head are missing.

In this particular case half of a head was missing. First crumple paper and press it into the remains of the head. Fashion it into the shape of the missing area in order to make a foundation on which to build.

It is only possible to do this to composition, china and pot heads. In the illustration we have used Milliput to build up a Bisque Dream Baby. When you are satisfied with the made up shape, lightly smear vaseline over the paper area. This will enable you to remove the paper when the head has been rebuilt. In this case Milliput was used but it would be possible to use other materials if these are preferred.

Mix Milliput in the usual way, so that it can be rolled out like a small piece of pastry. Ensure that you mix more Milliput than when you are using it as a filler. The piece rolled out will have to be slightly larger than the missing area of the head which must be covered completely. Smooth off the edges very carefully where the filler has overlapped onto the bisque. Remember that ridges are much harder to rub down when they are dry so the more time spent smoothing onto the bisque the easier it will be in the end.

Now that you have made the initial covering ensure that you are satisfied with the outline. When the Milliput is hard you can proceed to rub down and fill in where necessary, eg. on the joins and building up any indentations and holes. You will need a great deal of patience for this and the finish will have to be perfect before you can progress to glazing. As you can see the end result is most satisfactory and gives one a marvellous sense of achievement.

43. *The remaining half of a dream baby head*

44. *The head is stuffed with newspaper to make a good solid base ready for building up*

45. *The head after the layer of Milliput has been added and rubbed down*

46. *The finished head*

43

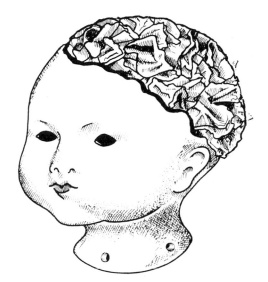

44

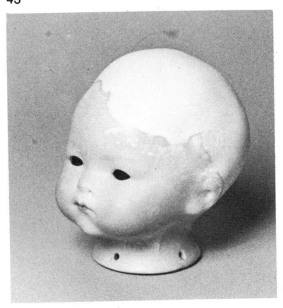

45

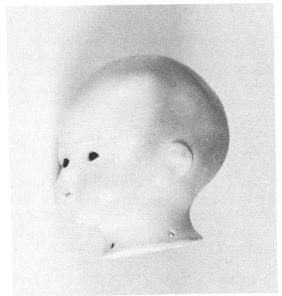

46

Example 2: Restoring a very badly repaired head.

It is not usual to have to work on a doll's head which has been as badly restored as the one illustrated here. None the less extreme cases arise from time to time and it is worth giving this doll some consideration as an example.

The bisque head had been glued together and then filled with cement. The result was not only a very bad finish but also an exceptionally heavy head. A bolt had also been embedded into the cement to enable the head to be fixed to the kid body. Fortunately this was never achieved and the body was still unspoilt and intact.

The only way to remove the bisque from the cement is to chip away the cement using a fine chisel and light hammer. Great care must be taken not to damage the bisque further while this is being done. Some small deposits of cement will be left on the bisque and these should be carefully scraped away when all the pieces have been separated and cleaned. When this has been done to your satisfaction the pieces can be glued together in the usual way, the cracks filled and missing pieces can be built up following the methods previously described.

Unfortunately the eyes, which are extremely brittle, cannot be salvaged in this instance. They remain embedded in the cement and new eyes have to be used.

While restoration of this type can give great satisfaction, it is also very costly both in time and materials. As a result it may well be better to try to find a replacement head than to pay a restorer to rebuild the old one.

47. *Note the cement filling inside the head*

48. *The bisque has been removed from the cement filler*

49. *The head restuck*

47

48

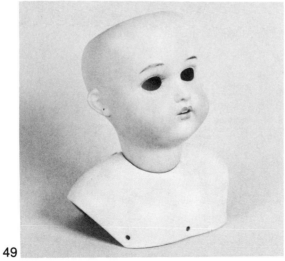

49

Repair of Bodies and Limbs

Composition Bodies

If the damage to a composition body is minimal a general purpose filler can be used for repairs. I prefer to use Milliput but I have also made satisfactory repairs with Polyfilla (fine surface filler). Damage on the body can either be an actual hole or an indentation which has cracked the surface. You will often find damage around the neck area and around the arm and leg sockets, such as joins and seams splitting and edges which have chipped. Clean any dirt away from the affected areas and then carefully apply the filler. This should then be left to dry overnight before it is rubbed down and retouched with paint.

Bodies can be extensively split and torn. This can be caused by too tight a restring, or the metal hooks or wires catching the body and cutting through it. Sockets are often enlarged where the material has broken away or the fibre or cardboard socket cups have disappeared entirely, (these are similar to head pates and in some instances they can be used if they have a hole in them).

If the edges are chewed and ragged and have lost their rigidity, trim them back to the good firm part so that you have something supportive to work from. With luck you may be able to fit the new cup and be able to glue it in to place. Fill the joins in the usual way. If too much of the socket has broken away measure the width of the hole and if possible a good socket so that you can calculate where to place the socket cup. You can check this by holding the cup in the hole and by placing the limb in it to ensure the correct position. Tape the socket

50. *Notice the damage around the arm and leg sockets*

51. *The cup is set into the worn and ripped leg socket and fixed with tape*

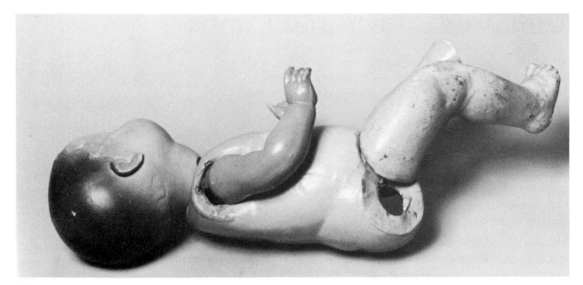

50

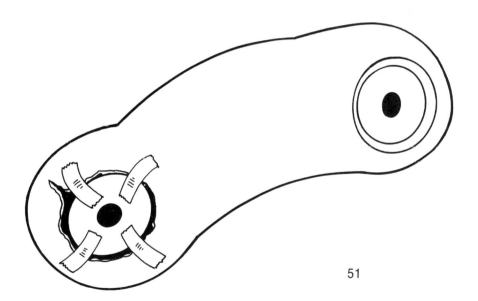

51

cup into place, fix the tape on the inside of the body and tape firmly so that when you commence to build up the hole the cup does not move. Masking tape is the most suitable for this job. Continue to fill hole with tape so that this will support the filler whilst it is drying. But be careful not to cover the hole which the elastic will pass through.

Mix your filler so that it is as near to the original material as possible i.e. paper and glue is paper maché (Polycel wallpaper glue is most useful), glue and sawdust or glue and cardboard, the cardboard should not be too thick. If you want to include a little pot finely grind down some flower pot clay using a pestle and mortar. Plaster can also be added in this way. It is as well to experiment first so that you will obtain the correct consistency.

It is difficult to give exact quantities as there is so much variety in the composition of bodies. Build up the filler gradually, let each application dry thoroughly, avoid making a too solid filler so that the repair becomes much heavier than the rest of the body, your experiments will help to avoid this. After the final application of filler rub down to make a fine smooth surface ready to receive the paint.

Bodies and limbs are easier to paint than china heads although you must again avoid any hard lines or brush strokes. This is more likely to be a problem when you are painting the repair only and trying to blend in with existing paint. You may find that although you have matched the colour successfully it looks too new; if this is the case lightly rub the new paint with a piece of newspaper allowing the newsprint to dirty the paint work. This must be done when the paint is dry but before you varnish it.

52. *A badly damaged body which will need to be built up*

53. *The body filled and now ready for rubbing down*

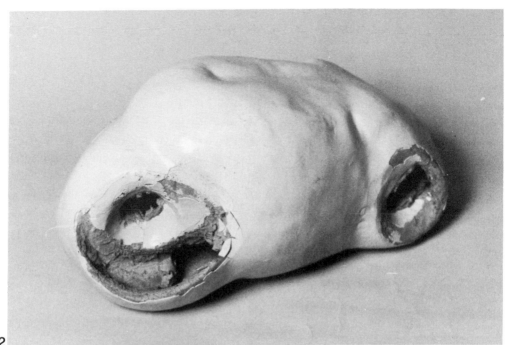

52

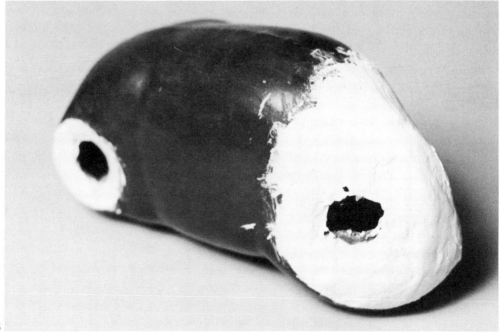

53

Composition Limbs

Fingers are often broken and new ones can be moulded in Milliput straight on to the broken part. If more than one finger is broken, it is advisable to mould one finger at a time. Remember to mark any dimples and nails before the Milliput drys. The same applies to toes. The restored limb can be propped up in sand to dry. If a whole limb is painted, you clearly cannot put it into the sand but you can suspend the limb by its hook from a wire coat hanger. You can then paint it and leave it to dry.

Hooks are often missing or loose. These can be replaced and fixed in with Milliput.

If for example part of the limb is missing (see illustration) it is best to crumple chicken wire (select gauge according to size of limb) in order to make a rough shape of the limb or foot or hand and press it into the hole in remaining part of the limb. Remember that you are going to cover this so make it slightly smaller than the actual size required. Cover the wire with an appropriate filler, rub it down and paint it as described earlier.

You may find it easier to make a hand or certainly the fingers alone from Milliput after the other filler has dried.

All the above instructions would apply to a painted body. **Jointed limbs** however have more sockets and they are smaller than on the baby bodies. You will also have to contend with ball joints which are always made of wood and are often missing. If you are a woodworker these can be turned on a lathe, but they can also be bought in spare part shops or at fairs. Alternatively wooden beads which can be purchased in craft shops can be used although this is usually a more expensive way of buying them.

54. *A broken limb. The foot has been built up with chicken wire*

55. *The above leg with filler partly applied. Milliput can be rolled out flat and pressed directly onto the wire. In this case plaster was more appropriate so the wire was covered with bandage before the plaster was applied*

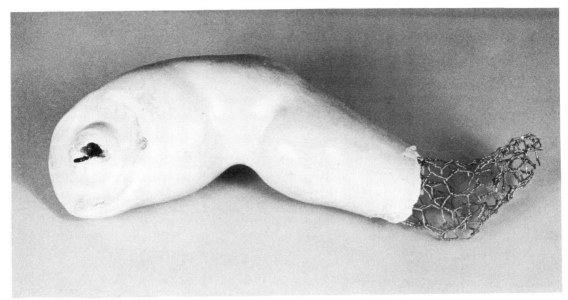

54

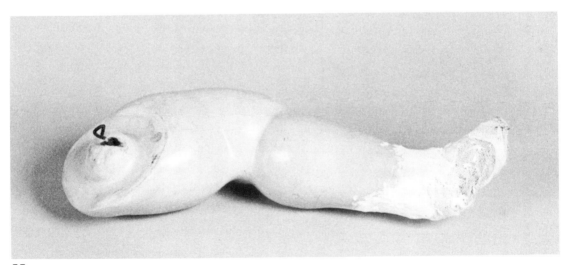

55

Wooden Bodies

We have previously discussed composition over wood; as the wood is protected by the composition it is unlikely that the wooden part will be damaged. However the Peg, Deutsch, or Dutch Dolls are entirely made of wood and these can be extensively damaged.

The wood from which these dolls are made is soft wood and is easier to work than hard wood. The head and body is quite solid and unlikely to have much damage except where the limbs fit onto body. These limbs are articulated and the joints are pinned with wood at the shoulders, elbows, base of body and knees. This is where damage most frequently occurs. If the peg part which holds the pin is damaged you will have to cut or saw the damaged piece out, make a new piece to fit and glue into place with evo-stick.

Frequently the pins are broken or missing. Wooden matchsticks make suitable pins for the smaller dolls and any suitable wood can be shaped to make pins for the larger dolls. Hands and feet are quite crude and are usually spade or paddle shape with no toes or fingers.

A good example of the crude wooden feet and hands are illustrated with a fabric body and wax head.

56. *A Deutsch doll, rather heavily clothed but showing the wooden head and wooden spade hands*

56

Kid Leather

It is possible to buy new leather from suppliers and in some instances there is no alternative but to use this to make repairs. I do however prefer used leather, providing it is in good condition and not rotting. The old leather is more suitable for patching and repairing as it blends in better with the existing body parts. The best source of supply for old leather is usually jumble sales or second hand clothing shops. A particularly useful source is old kid gloves.

If the damaged area consists of a hole or tear in the body or limb, the doll may also have lost an amount of sawdust stuffing. This will have to be replaced. Re-pack any of the old sawdust as tightly as possible, taking care not to further damage the leather covering and then add more sawdust where necessary. This can be obtained from wood yards and furniture restorers. But it must be extremely fine so remove any chips or shavings before inserting it.

Cut a piece of leather to the exact shape of the tear or hole and to the exact size so that the edges will fit flush. In this way you will avoid a bulky piece of leather heavily overlapping. Before gluing the leather patch into position place a small piece of fine cotton material over the hole, tucking it well under the edges of the leather. This will hold back the sawdust and provide a base to which the patch can be glued.

Apply glue to the leather patch covering it evenly but be careful not to use too much glue as it will ooze out when pressed onto fabric facing. Make certain that the edges of your patch are glued. If stitching is required on a seam use the same stitch that has already been used on the seam using a fine needle and cotton thread. Kid leather is very soft and supple and will tear easily so great care must be taken.

57. *A kid leather body in poor condition prior to repair*

58

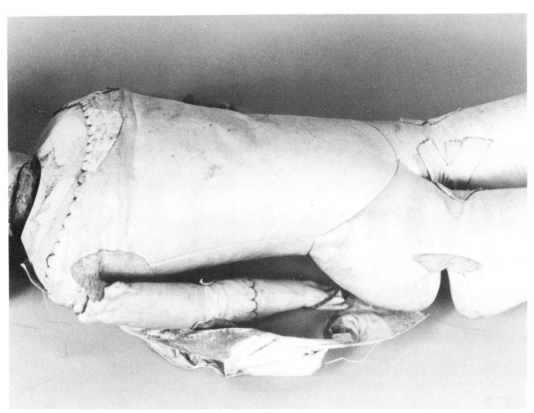

57

If the leather body is dirty it can be cleaned in the following way. Dip a small sponge into mild detergent, squeeze it out and clean small areas at a time. Do not soak the leather. If by mistake you do happen to do so leave it to dry before continuing. As you clean each section dry it thoroughly with a clean dry cloth.

Polish sparingly with any commercial white shoe polish and buff up with a clean soft cloth.

If you need to replace a limb or body, endeavour to take a pattern from the old part. (These parts can also be purchased ready made from suppliers as can patterns with instructions included). If you are taking a pattern from an old part, carefully unpick the seams noting which stitch and seam is used. Carefully save the sawdust filling for re-use. When the pieces are unpicked place them on brown paper, pin to secure and draw or cut out the pattern. Do not forget to mark where gussets and tucks occur. When you have made a satisfactory pattern place it onto the new leather and repeat the process. Clearly machine stitching is preferable but it is possible to hand stitch the parts if you prefer using a fine needle and cotton (not nylon).

Bisque or composition lower limbs should be repaired before they are fixed into the leather parts. Carefully glue the inside of the leather arm or leg, insert the bisque or composition part and bind it with tape until the glue is dry and the limb is fixed. The tape should then be removed. The head is finally attached in the same manner as the limbs.

58. *The patch for a kid body must be cut only very slightly smaller than the hole it is to fill in order that the edges meet but do not overlap*

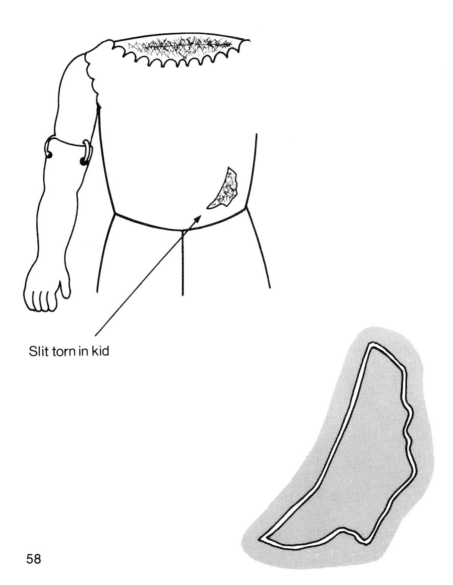

Slit torn in kid

Fabric Bodies

Fabric bodies are found on antique dolls and at the other extreme on some plastic and vinyl dolls.

Antique Fabric

You can obtain ready made fabric bodies or patterns in the same way as you can for kid bodies. Alternatively you can take a pattern from an old body as described in a previous chapter. They will be stuffed with sawdust. Retain all the old filling and add new filling if this is necessary.

The method of repairing will differ from the previous instruction for kid bodies which dealt with a hole or tear. In this case patching is necessary. Place a new piece of fabric over the hole, tucking the edges underneath the edges of the old fabric around the hole. This piece will of course need to be larger than the hole. Turn the edges of the hole under neatly and carefully glue these into place. I prefer not to stitch, because gluing is less obvious and the patch will be much neater.

There are many kinds of heads and limbs which are found on fabric bodies. They can be made of bisque, porcelain, celluloid, composition or wax but whatever the material they will have either a breast plate of a flange neck. The breast plated head will be glued on over the fabric body. Sometimes there is a small hole at each corner of the breast plate which enables the head to be stitched to the body. The flange head has a ridge round the neck to enable the body to be tied to the head using a draw string.

In the same way limbs can be stuck into the fabric or flanged and securely tied.

Any repairs necessary to head or limbs should be completed before fixing to the body.

59. *An old fabric body in a bad state of repair. As the fabric is rotten the body will have to be recovered using the old stuffing*

60. *An old fabric body showing very little wear except where the limbs join the fabric above the knee*

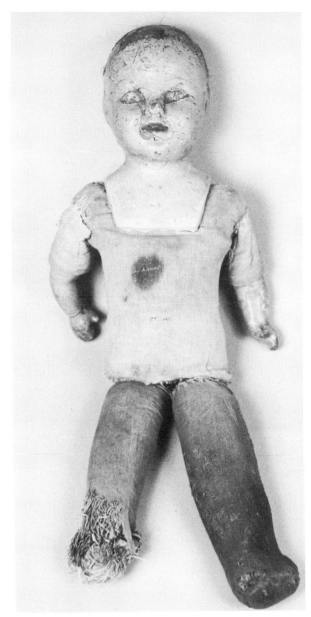

59

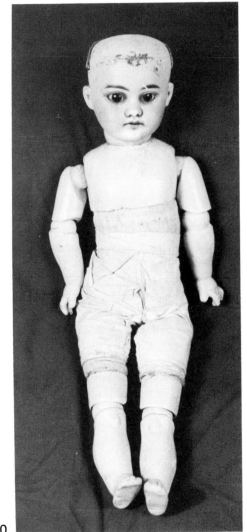

60

Modern Fabric

Some modern dolls have stuffed fabric bodies.
These unfortunately can come away from their
vinyl parts all too easily. In most cases the body
covering is too flimsy.

In order to produce a stronger doll take a
pattern from the old body and make the new
body in calico. This can be obtained in flesh
colour or ecru. Fix the limbs onto the body
before stuffing it and then replace the head. If
the limbs and neck are flanged use a draw
string of thin stringing elastic instead of cotton.
Pull this as tight as possible securing it with a
reef knot. The head and limbs will remain in
place using this method.

Some of the vinyl limbs and heads are
stitched to the fabric and this often breaks
away. In this case re-stitch it using the existing
holes and, for extra strength, paint a band of
copydex to fix the stitches. When this is dry
stick a band of tape over the top in order to
ensure a strong and tidy joint.

61.   A modern fabric body

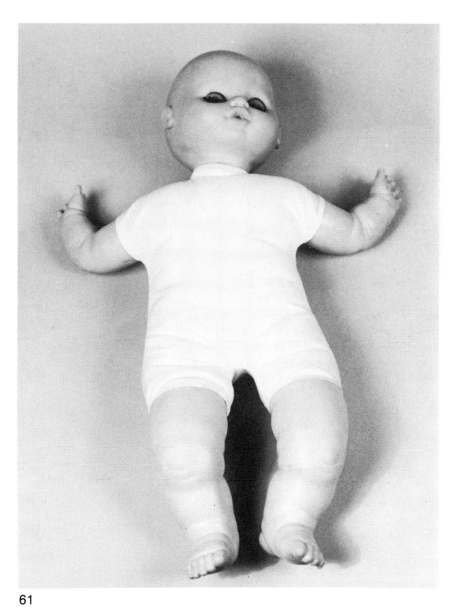

61

China Bodies

The limbs and bodies made of bisque or porcelain are repaired in the same manner as described for china heads. Bond, fill in with Milliput and rub down to make a fine smooth surface for painting and reglazing.

Because limbs are often of an awkward shape for gluing it is likely that plasticine or a tray of sand will be needed to support the limbs while the glue is drying.

62.   Small china bodies

Wax Bodies and Limbs

It is seldom that you come across a wax body. Many dolls do however have wax limbs. Repairs must be done with caution following the same method as described for wax heads.

If you wish to attempt to make limbs you can try carving solid limbs from a block of wax which is not easy. Alternatively the wax may be warmed and moulded by hand.

Another alternative is to pour liquid wax into a mould, made of plasticine, latex or plaster, which has been formed on a similar limb. You will need to experiment with wax and learn by experience. The most suitable waxes to use are paraffin, beeswax and candle wax which can be mixed together to obtain a combination of wax which you find good to work with and which matches the wax previously used.

You may find it easier to make the limbs in papier maché or composition and then dip them in the fluid wax.

A wood glue should be used for any gluing that is required.

62

Vinyl and Plastic

There is not a lot one can do to repair these materials. But it is worth mentioning that limbs can be replaced. Although new ones are unobtainable it is still possible to find old dolls at jumble sales from which parts can be taken.

It may be necessary to replace both arms and legs, as it is unlikely that you will find an exact match for the existing limb. In this case remove both the good limb as well as the damaged one. Steam from a kettle will soften the vinyl to make removal easier and avoid undue strain on the doll.

The new limbs can be placed into the body by the same method. When the plastic cools it will return to its rigid state holding the limbs firmly into place.

63. A vinyl body

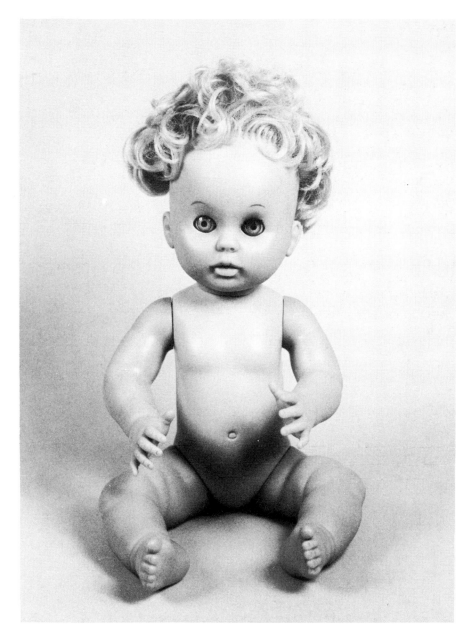

63

Restringing

Special doll elastic is bought in various thicknesses, and it is easy to select the most suitable because the principles are the same for straight or bent limb bodies. Make sure that the hooks are securely embedded and fix them with Milliput if they are not.

To avoid the danger of the head being broken if it is dropped, always cover your table with a folded towel when restringing a doll.

Measure the elastic approximately to double the length of the body. Place through the hook at the neck of the head. Then continue to thread both ends through the neck of body. Bring an end out through each leg opening in the body and hook on the legs to both ends of the elastic. Pull the elastic tight so that the head and legs are firmly in place and finish off with a reef knot. It is then possible with the aid of a button hook to pull out through the arm hole a piece of elastic and so hook on an arm. Repeat this with the other arm.

Sometimes when the arms are strung this way on one piece of elastic they do not sit correctly. This may be due to the shape or size of the arm hole or position of hooks. If this is a problem I prefer to string the arms separately. Measure the elastic against the width of the body, thread it through the hook of one arm then both ends through the armholes. Hook on the second arm, pull it tight and finish with a reef knot.

64. *A five piece baby or toddler body showing the stringing inside*

65. *A body ready for restringing*

66. *A restrung body. The head will fit securely over the bar at the neck*

70

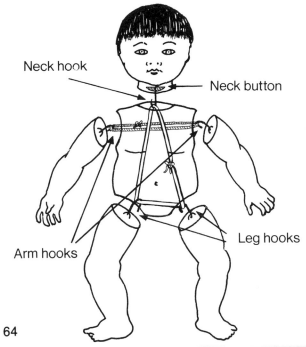

Neck hook

Neck button

Arm hooks

Leg hooks

64

THE REEF KNOT:

Right over left, left over right

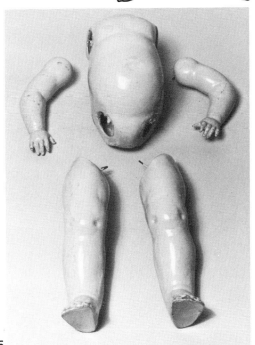

65

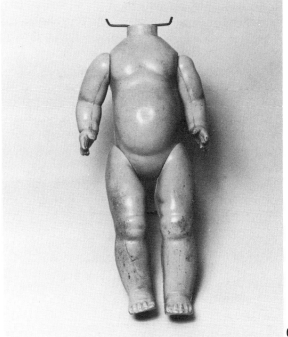

66

Celluloid Bodies

Some celluloid bodies are conventional having arm holes and leg holes and limbs which have a built in lug with a hole for restringing. This can be done as previously described but take care not to string celluloid bodies too tightly and cause splits.

The other design for celluloid bodies (illustration 67) has to be strung somewhat differently. I still prefer to start with the head as before. Again threading elastic through the body and bringing each end through the two leg openings. Thread the elastic through the discs, tighten it to the correct tension and finish with a large enough knot so that it does not slip through the hole in the disc. These are split to the hole so that you can squeeze them to make them smaller in order to fit in to the opening on the limb. When you release the pressure they spring back to the original size fitting snugly and holding the limb in place.

If any of discs are missing you can make new ones out of celluloid (or plastic would suffice). Cut your disc slightly larger than the hole in the limb, make one cut to the centre and make a hole in the centre of the disc large enough for the elastic to thread through.

The most common damage found on these bodies and limbs are splits which usually occur around arm holes, neck or leg holes. These are best welded together by melting the edges of the celluloid with acetone as previously described.

67. *Celluloid parts ready to be restrung, showing the discs split to the centre so that they can be adjusted to fit the limbs*

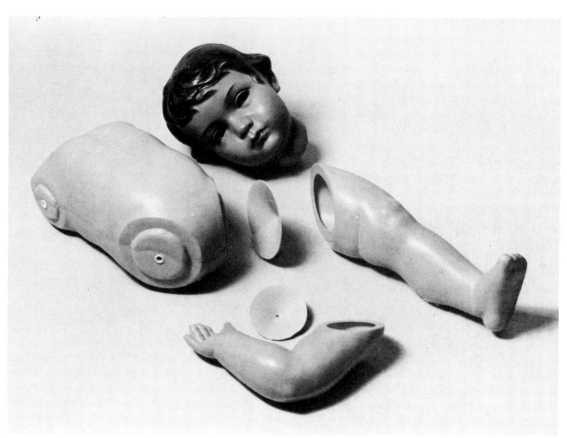

67

Jointed Dolls

The body and limbs of jointed dolls can have as many as thirteen pieces. All of these have to be strung in the correct order. It is very easy to place the right hand on the left side or vice-versa and the legs in particular can cause trouble, especially the upper parts. It is advisable to lay them out in order before you start to restring. (illustration 68).

Study the lower limbs first as this is where you will commence to restring and also where you can experience a major problem. If a hook or a bar is firmly embedded in the socket of the lower limb, enabling you to thread your elastic then the re-string will be straight forward. However it may be that the ball joint is firmly embedded into the socket of the lower limb with no apparent means of holding the elastic. Unfortunately this ball joint has to be removed. Do not be tempted to break it off as you may break the plaster around the edge of the socket.

Carefully cut into the thin layer of plaster which is holding the ball joint in the leg socket and gently release it. You should find a small pin recessed and glued into the ball joint ready for threading the elastic. If you have to replace the pin make sure you use wire or a pin that will not bend, and clean out any old glue from the recess. Reglue the pin in place and ensure that the glue has thoroughly dried before starting to restring.

Measure your elastic against the body and limbs as before except this time you must use it double and of a thinner gauge. You can string from left to right or right to left whichever you prefer. Thread the elastic through the ball joint and over the pin, keeping the two ends level and pass the elastic double thread through the upper limb, through the body, (a button hook is most useful for this job) and out through

68. *A jointed body ready to be restrung*

69. *A correctly strung jointed body*

74

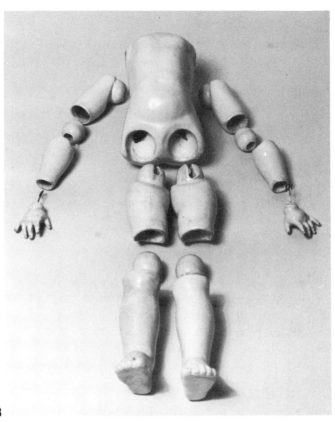

68

69

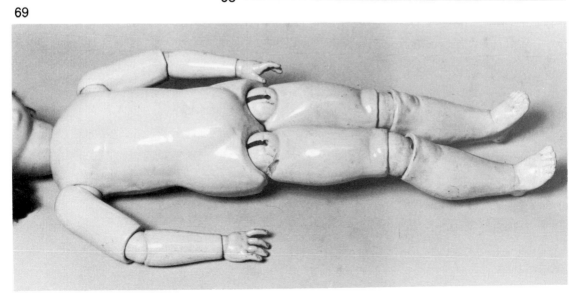

neck hole. Next hook on head, pass the elastic back through the neck and down the body and out through the opposite leg hole; through the upper limb and then through the other ball joint. Finally tie the elastic securely over the pin when the correct tension is obtained. Using wood glue you must stick the lower limbs onto the ball joints and make good the crack by filling in and repainting.

Restring the arms starting at one hand and using double elastic to thread through the sections then through the body and down through the sections of the other arm finishing at the hand and tie securely.

70. *The seventeen piece jointed body doll*

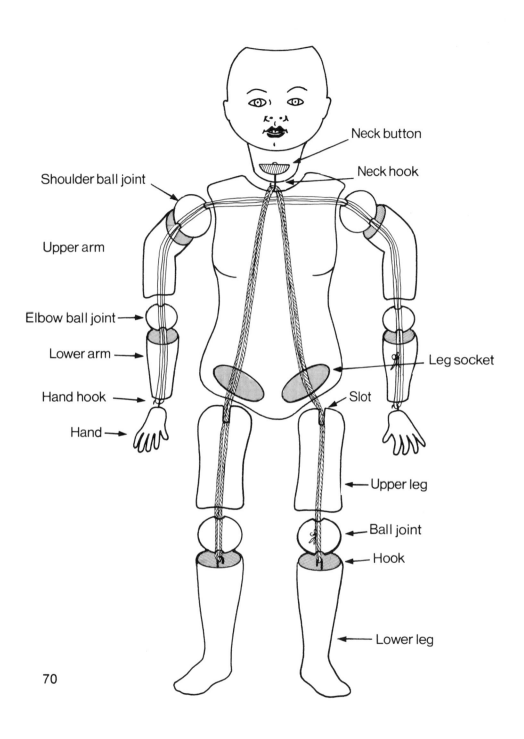

Neck button

Neck hook

Shoulder ball joint

Upper arm

Elbow ball joint

Lower arm

Hand hook

Hand

Leg socket

Slot

Upper leg

Ball joint

Hook

Lower leg

70

Pincushion Dolls or Half Dolls

These dolls are entirely different from those previously mentioned but are avidly collected by many enthusiasts.

They are mostly found in their half state, because the fabrics that made up the lower half would have long ago perished. They are found in many sizes and when complete they would have been crinolined ladies elegantly covering tea pots and such like and even, occasionally they are found as lamp shades. They were also made into pin cushions which can still be found wholly intact.

It is still possible to buy these dolls for a few pounds, although one does see much more expensive ones at doll & antique fairs. Quite often they are damaged which makes them cheaper to buy, and with the same loving care they can be restored to their former glory.

The most valuable dolls are usually made in fine porcelain and beautifully glazed. The German makers of fine porcelain excelled in making these particular dolls and Japan also manufactured them. The Japanese quality was not as good but they are still very collectable.

Many half dolls were made in bisque and had moulded hair or mohair. They would have had articulated or fixed arms. More recent dolls have been made in plaster which are quite nice to own as they are usually fashioned in the styles of the thirties.

Damage is often found round the base and was probably broken when detached from the fabric. This damage can be repaired with Milliput in the same way as described earlier in the book – building up and rubbing down. Do

71. *Perfect pincushion dolls in the style of the 1930s*

72. *German pincushion dolls depicting classical styles*

71

72

not forget to pierce the holes in the base before the Milliput hardens. These holes were originally there to facilitate the stitching of the doll to the fabric. This part is not usually glazed because it is embedded into the fabric.

Arms are quite often broken; if you are good at modelling these can be made separately and glued on. The join then must be filled in as described in the chapter on filling and building up. Alternatively you can mould Milliput directly on to the broken piece of the doll. If this method is used it is advisable to model over a metal pin (see illustration). Attach the arm with Milliput and leave it to dry hard. Then build up with the Milliput. Care must be taken when rubbing down as it is extremely easy to snap off the new piece.

Other damage can be found to the hair especially pompadour styles, also to hats, feathers and stand up collars. You should repair these with Milliput by filling in the moulding to match the shape or pattern. Remember to mark any pattern or ridges before the Milliput hardens.

Heads are sometimes broken off. These may be replaced and stuck with Araldite. The position of head is usually angled so it will need support until it is absolutely dry. Support the head or for that matter arms with plasticine.

Fill in at the join and rub down in the usual way and re-glaze. Humbrol enamels are most suitable for these dolls. In the case of bisque painting and glazing rules apply as for bisque headed dolls mentioned in previous chapters.

These half dolls look charming in a glass cabinet and usually look more effective as a collection than mixed with other types of dolls.

73. *Pincushion dolls as they are received for repair*

74. *A complete pincushion doll but with hands still to be repaired*

73

74

Clothing

It is seldom that the original clothes are found on these old dolls, and if they are, they are usually rotten, badly marked and extremely dirty or dusty. The under garments are often in better condition as the dress will have taken the brunt of wear and tear for a great many years.

Cleaning and Washing

First of all remove any stains before washing the garments. The most likely stains are ironmould, rust and mildew.

Ironmould

This can be removed from cotton and linen with salts of lemon. Sprinkle the salts onto the stain and pour boiling water over it. For wool and silk use a solution of Hyposulphite Bleach.

Rust

All materials can be treated with salts of sorrel.

Mildew

This is one of the hardest stains to get rid of. Use either Hydrogen Peroxide or salts of sorrel solution. This is suitable for cotton and linen. For wool and silk use Permanganate of Potash. Do not be alarmed when you find that this has turned the stain brown, you now treat this with peroxide.

75. *A beautifully clothed Victorian Deutsch doll showing the bustle effect of the skirt*

Ink

One does occasionally come across ink stains; these can sometimes be removed with milk. However if the stains are stubborn cotton and linen can be treated with lemon juice and salt followed by pouring boiling water over it. Wool and silk treat as above for mildew.

The peroxide solution should be as follows: 1 part peroxide, 1 part vinegar, 4 parts water.

When washing the clothes it is important to avoid colour runs. These old clothes are not usually colour fast so it is necessary to test this before immersing them in water. The test can be made by damping an unobtrusive piece of the garment and pressing it onto a white paper towel. If the garments are not colour fast they can only be dry cleaned or left as they are.

Washable clothes should only be washed very gently in something like stergene or soap flakes (not strong detergents). Squeeze them very gently and rinse them in the same way. Dry them flat on a clean towel. Iron carefully with a warm iron, and do be careful not to catch the point of the iron in arm folds etc. as the material will easily rip.

Some materials are not suitable for washing as previously mentioned. Some wool and flannel may shrink. Velveteen should be steamed. Watered silk loses its pattern. But all of these will dry clean suitably.

Repairs

Small repairs can be executed quite successfully but remember to use cotton and not nylon thread for sewing. Ribbons that need replacing can be aged before fixing to the garment and this can be effected by washing it several times. Try to amass a stock of old buttons which will always be useful. Jumble sales and fairs are a good source for these.

76. *Underclothes in the traditional style*

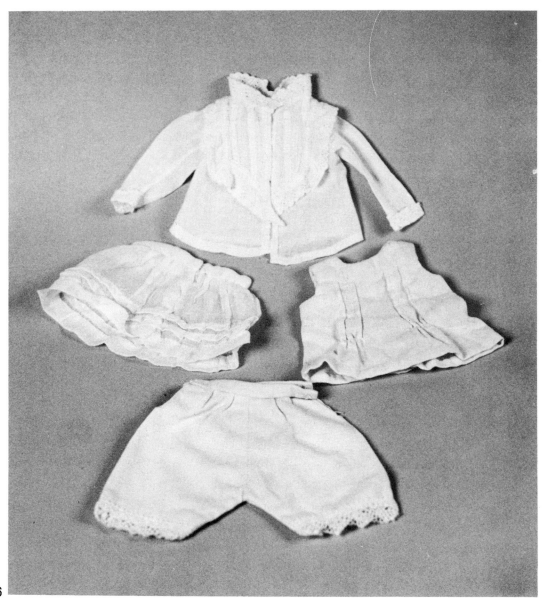

New Clothes

There are many books on this subject which will give detail patterns and instructions. As this book is on repair and restoration I will mention new clothes only briefly.

Do take care to use compatible material. New materials can be aged by washing, and only natural fibres should be used. One can hunt at fairs, jumble sales and Oxfam shops for old materials but it is necessary to ensure that they are sound. Remember to use cotton sewing thread, non plastic buttons and fasteners.

Do keep in proportion with the doll such things as trimmings, buttons and fasteners.

77. *Examples of traditional style clothes made up in old materials*

77

Materials and Suppliers

There are many materials which are used by professional restorers. These are difficult to obtain unless you are in the trade. I am therefore only mentioning materials that are both perfectly adequate, and also easy to buy and use.

Spare Parts
Elastic (various thickness)
Ready made hooks to fit in limbs
or pliable wire to make your own
Glass eyes (new ones)
Head domes of cork and fibre
Fibre neck cones
Mohair
Teeth
Tongues
Eye Lashes
Real Hair Wigs

M. Wanke UK Ltd
29 London Road,
Bexhill on Sea,
East Sussex.
Tel: 0424 223291

Rock a By Dolly
75 Pound Street,
Carshalton, SM5 4HA
Tel: 01-647 6155

Human Hair wefting
for making or restoring wigs

Stanparis
239 Mile End Road,
London E1.
Tel: 01-790 3996

Eyes for composition and vinyl dolls
wigs, mohair, neck cones, head domes
hooks, glass eyes

Bella Hajos Ltd
240 Old London Road,
Hastings,
East Sussex. TN34 3NS
Tel: 0424 428381

Adhesives
Evostick or wood glue
Best for composition wax or wood dolls
Standard Araldite
Plastic Padding, Super Epoxy Glue (fast drying)
for Bisque or Porcelain
Copydex
for wigs & fabric

Any D.I.Y Shop
    or
Green & Stone
259 Kings Road,
Chelsea SW3
Tel: 01-352 0837

Fillers
Milliput
for moulding & filling in
Polyfilla fine surface filler
Tetrion fine fill   D.I.Y Shops
Dental plaster
for resetting eyes & filling in fine surfaces,
Papier Mache (paste and paper)
for mending limbs & bodies

The Milliput Co.
Unit 5 Marian Mawr.
Dolgllan Gwynedd,
Mid Wales. LL40 1UU
Tel: 0341 422562
or Green & Stone
Chelsea, or Rock a By
Dolly

Paints & Glazes Solvents
White Spirit
Cellulose thinners   for mixing with paints & glaze
Methylated spirit   for cleaning surfaces etc.
Humbrol Enamels, matt flesh colours & glaze
Powdered Pigments to be used with glaze
to make flesh tints
Titanium white, yellow ochre, cadmium yellow
Orange chrome, crimson alizum raw sienna
Burnt sienna, Raw umber, Burnt umber
Rusting plastic coatings, white matt & gloss
to be used with powdered pigments, Humbrol paint
and silk emulsion match pots
Crown silk emulsion match pots
Green lily, Bracken leaf, Tea Rose, Sweet Briar,
Pale Chestnut, Country Beige, Magnolia

Green & Stone
254 Kings Road,
Chelsea SW3
Tel: 01-352 0837

or D.I.Y Shops

Tools

Hooking tools of various lengths
(old button hooks are most suitable) (junk shops)
Sharp scissors
Painted pliers
Old forceps   (junk shops)
Steel Spatulas Nos. 47 & 48

New items from
M. Wanke UK Ltd
29 London Road,
Bexhill on Sea,
East Sussex.
or
A. Tirante
Goodge Place, W1

Scalpels Nos. 3 & 4
Paint Brushes (sable)
Nos. 0, 1, 2, 3
Air Brush & Compressor (optional)

Green & Stone

Material for taking moulds

Plasticine (natural or white colour)
Latex Rubber
Latex Thickener
fine sawdust (for thickening latex)
Cotton Buds
Dental plaster
Wire
Titanium Dioxide Powder Pigment
Liquid Araldite 103–956

Green & Stone

Self curing modelling plastic

Aesthelic Productions
111 Tudor Ave.,
Worcester Park,
Surrey.
Tel: 01-337 0283

Sundry materials

Abrasive Papers Fine 2 & Wet & Dry
Sellotape
White French Chalk
Kitchen Roll
China Paint Palettes
Porcelain Plain tiles
Nitromors or Paint Stripper
Bowl or Deep Pan of silver sand

D.I.Y. Shops

Wax for setting eyes	**M. Wanke**
Bees-wax for doll repair Sticky wax	**Green & Stone**
Weights	**Fishing tackle shops**

Doll Collections

It is very useful for the restorer to visit doll collections in order to see some of the rarer dolls in relatively good conditions. The more that you see dolls in good and correct condition the more likely you are to restore them sympathetically.

I have listed below some collections which I have enjoyed visiting.

The Bethnal Green Museum of Childhood.
(A large collection of dolls and other toys of all periods).
Cambridge Heath Road, London, E2 9PA.

Pollocks Toy Museum.
1 Scala Street, London, W.1.
(A variety of toys and dolls).

The Precinct Toy Collection.
38 Harnet Street, Sandwich.
(A small private collection with some very good examples of dolls).

The Lilliput Museum of Antique Dolls and Toys.
High Street, Brading. I.O.W.
(A private collection of old dolls with some houses and toys).

The Burrows Toy Museum.
The Octagon, 46 Milson Street, Bath.

Museum of Childhood
Water Street, Menai Bridge, Anglesey, Gwymedd.
(A comprehensive collection of toys, pastimes, and dolls).

The Toy Museum.
The Grange, Rottingdean, Sussex.
(A small but interesting collection).

Arundel Toy & Military Museum.
Dolls House Toy Museum,
23 High Street, Arundel,
West Sussex, BN18 9AD
(A delightful collection of
nursery bygones)

Further Reading

There are several good books on dolls and doll restoration and I
have listed below some which I have read and found useful in my
work.

How to Repair and Dress Old Dolls.
   by Audry Johnson published by Bell and Hyman

The Handbook of Doll Repair and Restoration
   by Marty Westfall published by Robert Hale

The Jumeau Doll.
   by Margaret Whitton published in U.S.A. by Dover Publications
   Inc.

European and American Dolls.
   by Gwen White published by B. T. Batsford Ltd.

The Collectors Encyclopaedia of Dolls
   by D. S., E. A. and E. J. Coleman published by Crown Publishing,
   New York.